The **Essential** Buyer's Guide

MAZDA

RX-8

All models 2003 to 2012

Your marque expert:
Julian Parish

VELOCE PUBLISHING
THE PUBLISHER OF FINE AUTOMOTIVE BOOKS

www.veloce.co.uk

For post publication news, updates and amendments relating to this book please visit www.veloce.co.uk/books/V4867

First published in April 2016 by Veloce Publishing Limited, Veloce House, Parkway Farm Business Park, Middle Farm
Way, Poundbury, Dorchester, Dorset, DT1 3AR, England.
Fax 01305 250479/e-mail info@veloce.co.uk/web www.veloce.co.uk or www.velocebooks.com.

ISBN: 978-1-845848-67-5 UPC: 6-36847-04867-9

Introduction
– the purpose of this book

The place of Mazda's RX-8 in history is assured. At its introduction in 2003, it was the latest in a line of rotary-engined cars from Mazda, starting with the Cosmo 110S in 1967. In 2015, Mazda's RX-Vision concept was the star of the Tokyo Motor Show, but for now the RX-8 is the last production rotary-engined car from any manufacturer.

The author's Velocity Red RX-8.

It is the rotary engine which makes the RX-8 so special, but also divides opinion like few others. Enthusiasts either love it or just don't get it. The rotary or Wankel engine (named after its German inventor, Felix Wankel) replaces the usual pistons with a triangular rotor, which spins inside an oval-shaped housing. The power generated by the rotor is applied to an eccentric shaft, which works in a way similar to the crankshaft in a conventional piston engine. Most production rotary engines – like the Renesis (Rotary Engine Genesis) fitted to the RX-8 – have two rotors.

Compared to conventional piston engines, the Renesis unit has far fewer moving parts, ensuring the extraordinary smoothness and willingness to rev for which rotary engines are renowned. In 2003 and 2004 it was chosen as World Engine of the Year. Its compact dimensions keep weight down and contribute to the car's low centre of gravity. Combined with the RX-8's all-round double-wishbone suspension and

One of the rotors inside its housing. (Courtesy Mazda)

sophisticated Torsen limited-slip differential, this layout makes for a great-handling car.

Whereas all three generations of the RX-7 were close-coupled two-door coupés, the RX-8 had an innovative body design, with so-called 'Freestyle' or 'suicide' rear doors, hinged at the rear and without a central pillar, which allow easy access to the surprisingly roomy rear seats. The combination of driving pleasure, practicality and excellent value made the RX-8 a compelling proposition when new, and the UK's *What Car?* magazine voted it Best Coupé three years running.

Ten years on, the picture is rather different. Some drivers could not come to terms with the rotary engine's relative lack of low-down torque, its tendency to flood when cold and its high fuel consumption. More importantly still, for would-be owners today, the rotary engine has acquired an unfortunate reputation for problems with worn apex seals and stationary gear bearings, which make replacing or rebuilding it almost inevitable. As a result, many cars are now off the road, and secondhand prices have plummeted.

Despite this, you don't have to be mad to want an RX-8 today! There is a tremendous network of enthusiasts and specialists who can keep an RX-8 running well, and some great bargains to be found. This book will guide you through all the points to check when viewing an RX-8, and help you make the right decision.

Thanks

I could not have prepared this guide without the enthusiastic support of the RX-8 community. I would particularly like to thank Owen Mildenhall (Mazda UK), Ben Dunn (Rotary Revs), Patrick Dwyer (TW White & Sons), Jean-Paul Soupizet and Kevin Pierre (SA Soupizet), Julien Manzi (Euro des Nations) and the UK Mazda RX-8 Owners' Club. As ever, my thanks are also due to the great team at Veloce Publishing, and especially to Rod Grainger, Kevin Quinn and Lizzie Bennett.

Julian Parish

The 'Freestyle' doors opened up.

Contents

The Essential Buyer's Guide™ currency
At the time of publication a BG unit of currency "●" equals approximately
£1.00/US$1.43/Euro 1.32. Please adjust to suit current exchange rates
using Sterling as the base currency.

1 Is it the right car for you?
– marriage guidance

Tall and short drivers
Most drivers should be comfortable, although the wheel adjusts only for rake, and some may find the gearlever set too far back. On RHD cars, there is limited space to rest your left foot. For tall drivers, the optional sunroof reduces headroom by 75mm (3in).

Weight of controls
The electric power steering and all controls are light and easy to use. Driving smoothly can be hard at first, however, due to the long clutch travel and light flywheel, which means that the revs drop away quickly.

Will it fit the garage?
Length:	175in	4435mm
Width:	70in	1770mm
Height:	53in	1340mm

The front seats of a late-model R3.
(Courtesy Mazda)

Interior space
The RX-8 is a genuine four-seater, with easy access and comfortable space for two adults in the rear. Standard Isofix mounting points make it simple to fit a child seat, and six airbags contribute to the car's safety. The rear is strictly for two though, thanks to the wide central tunnel, and the view out is limited.

Luggage capacity
At 2.9m^3 (10.2ft^3), the Mazda's luggage compartment is comparable to that of a small hatchback, with adequate space for two sets of golf clubs or weekend trips away. The opening is narrow, however, making it better suited to soft bags or carry-on luggage. The rear seat doesn't fold, but you can remove the storage compartment in the middle of the rear seat to create a 'ski hatch' for long items.

Running costs
The RX-8's fuel consumption is often exaggerated, but still high. Budget on 20-25mpg (Imp)/17-21mpg (US), more if driven hard or in cities. The rotary engine is designed to use oil (to lubricate the rotor seals), but again reports often exaggerate this; many owners achieve one litre (or US quart) per 2000 miles or more.

Usability
A practical car for four people on long trips, but the rotary engine needs to warm up, making it ill-suited to frequent cold starts and short journeys.

Parts availability

All service parts are readily available from Mazda dealers or independent specialists. Some specialist tools, including the rotary compression tester, are harder to come by.

Parts cost

Parts are no more expensive than for many conventional sports cars. The Bilstein shock absorbers fitted to models such as the PZ or 40th Anniversary are more expensive than the standard items, as are the tyres fitted to the 19in wheels on the R3.

Easy access to front and rear. (Courtesy Mazda)

Insurance

Members of RX-8 owners' groups usually enjoy preferential rates with specialist insurers, so check there first, and be sure to include track day use if required.

Investment potential

Definitely not. Just enjoy the fun of driving it!

Foibles

Take care not to flood the engine, if you have to switch it off when it is still cold. Run the engine at 3000rpm for 10-15 seconds, before returning it to idle and switching it off. This will purge unburned fuel from the combustion chambers.

Plus points

Unrivalled smoothness of the engine.
9000rpm redline (on 230 models).
Crisp gearchange.
Direct steering and enjoyable handling.
Space and comfort for four.

Minus points

Modest torque, limiting acceleration at lower revs.
Engine note.
High fuel consumption.
Lack of rigidity on rough surfaces.
Sensitivity to side winds.
Rear ¾ visibility.

Alternatives

Alfa Romeo GT, Audi TT, BMW 3-Series Coupé, Chrysler Crossfire, Honda S2000, Nissan 350Z, VW Scirocco.

Removable stowage unit giving access to the luggage compartment.

2 Cost considerations
– affordable, or a money pit?

Purchase price
In the UK especially, the RX-8 can be picked up at ridiculously cheap prices. But those cheap prices are usually for a reason, so be ready to budget for extensive mechanical work, and possibly a complete engine rebuild or replacement (see Chapter 13).

Servicing
In North America, some RX-8s will still be covered by Mazda's extended powertrain warranty (8 years/100,000 miles) and can be serviced in the official dealer network. In Europe, however, rotary expertise at Mazda's dealers is increasingly scarce; finding a good independent rotary specialist will usually be your best bet (see Chapter 16).

Oil change: every 6000 miles (9600km) recommended.
Service: at least every 12,500 miles (20,000km).

Parts prices
The prices opposite are for approved Mazda OEM parts; be wary of cheaper third-party parts, especially for the engine, unless they have been developed by a known rotary specialist. In the UK alone, 1000 cars are being broken for parts every year, so there is a good supply of used parts.

First-generation engine with plastic cover removed. (Courtesy Mazda)

Mechanical parts
Sparkplugs (each) ●x30
Ignition coils (each) ●x90
Battery ●x80
Starter motor ●x340
Coolant expansion tank ●x140
Oil cooler lines ●x100
Oil radiator ●x660
Water pump ●x70
Clutch assembly ●x290
Catalytic converter ●x1140
Exhaust back box ●x520
Replacement engine ●x3400
Brake discs/rotors (pair; front) ●x270
Brake discs/rotors (pair; rear) ●x140
Brake pads (pair; front) ●x70
Brake pads (pair; rear) ●x40
Front anti-roll bar drop links (pair) ●x90
Front suspension bushes (set) ●x70
Shock absorber (front; standard) ●x220
Shock absorber (rear; standard) ●x150
Shock absorber (front; Bilstein – PZ) ●x460
Shock absorber (rear; Bilstein – PZ) ●x360
Tyre (18in) from ●x120
Tyre (19in) from ●x130

Body parts
Bonnet (aluminium) ●x280
Front bumper ●x210
Rear bumper ●x240
Front door ●x250
Front wing ●x150
Windscreen ●x100
Rear screen ●x260
Alloy wheel (18in) ●x210
Xenon headlight ●x490
Tail light assembly ●x110
Tyre repair kit (with compressor) ●x100

Rear suspension assembly.
(Courtesy Mazda)

Front discs are much
more expensive than rear.
(Courtesy Mazda)

'Freestyle' rear door.
(Courtesy Mazda)

3 Living with an RX-8
– will you get along together?

Good points

The rotary engine defines the experience of driving the RX-8. Unrivalled for its smoothness, it will rev like a motorbike to over 9000rpm (in the higher-powered 230 versions). Use that rev range to the full, and the acceleration is decent enough,

9000rpm redline on second-generation US-market RX-8. (Courtesy Mazda)

with 0-60mph (96km/h) taking around seven seconds.

The light engine is located low down and behind the front axle line, guaranteeing a low centre of gravity and near-perfect 50:50 weight distribution. In turn, this ensures a low polar moment of inertia and excellent handling. Strong brakes, switchable traction control, a good gearchange (especially the six-speed), and direct steering (using electric assistance, long

before that became commonplace to save fuel) all contribute to a great drive. It's no wonder that the RX-8 has become a popular choice for track days.

Away from the track or country backroads, the RX-8 is an unexpectedly practical and comfortable companion, with room for four. Inside and out, the styling is unique. Above town speeds, the ride is surprisingly comfortable, helped by supportive seats on all models. The low noise levels at steady speeds, and high-quality Bose audio system

RX-8 on track in UK race series. (Courtesy Mazda)

Comfortable seats for four, here in an Evolve limited edition. (Courtesy Mazda)

make the RX-8 a good cruiser on the motorway or freeway.

Looking after any rotary-engined car demands commitment, and the RX-8 is no exception. Engine apart, however, the rest of the car is as reliable as many other Japanese models or conventional sports cars of its age. Many problems – including some related to the engine – were fixed on the second-generation models, or through dealer recalls to the earlier cars.

Bad points

The rotary engine makes and breaks the experience of driving an RX-8. When you don't want to rev it out (or simply find yourself in too high a gear to overtake), the lack of torque low down and in the mid-range can be frustrating. The lower-powered 190 versions actually have slightly more torque, but still need 4000rpm to come alive, the 230 versions closer to 6000rpm, as the secondary and – on 230 engines – auxiliary ports come into operation. Slick as the gearchange is, the narrow power band means that you'll be using it a lot. You'll be stopping for fuel frequently too, with consumption of at least 20-25mpg (Imp)/17-21mpg (US) to be expected, more if you drive hard or in cities. High CO_2 emissions (from 267 to 299g/km) won't impress your environmentally-minded friends.

The RX-8 engine has become notorious for its tendency to flood if turned off when cold. In over 21,000 miles (34,000km), the author never experienced this problem, but you do need to be aware of it, and let the engine warm through properly, or rev it to 3000rpm for 10-15 seconds before switching it off. Problems with the durability of the rotary engine are described in detail in Chapter 9.

To make the most of the RX-8's chassis, you may want to look for a PZ limited edition or later R3 car. Some drivers of first-generation cars have complained that there was some body flex on rough surfaces and a bit too much body roll. Grip is fantastic in the dry, rather less so in the wet, especially with the original Bridgestone RE040 tyres. And don't even think of taking an RX-8 with those tyres on snow! If you do a lot of motorway or freeway miles, the RX-8 is slightly sensitive to side winds, although it is no worse than many other cars in this regard.

Inside the cabin, the view towards the rear three-quarters is hindered by the broad pillars. If you live in a very hot climate, the air-conditioning may not be powerful enough, although Mazda did offer a so-called amplifier kit when the car was new. The piano black and aluminium trim lift the appearance inside the car. The materials used are generally robust, but there is a lot of hard plastic and the perceived quality is lower than on the premium German brands. You'd better like the rotary shape too, as it is everywhere, from the gearlever to the head restraints, from the seat adjusters to the rear foglamp!

The Renesis rotary engine. (Courtesy Mazda)

Summary

The RX-8 is what the British might call a 'Marmite' car. You'll either love it and its high-revving engine, and will be ready to nurture it like the future classic it is fast becoming, or you'll hate the effort required to enjoy it to the full. If you come to the Mazda from another Japanese car like the VTEC-engined Hondas, the switch to a rotary will probably be easy. If your last car had a turbocharged engine with lots of low-down torque, however, making the transition may be much harder.

4 Relative values
– which model for you?

Mazda only ever offered the RX-8 in one body style, so your choices will come down to the age of the car, its engine and transmission.

First generation or second?

Most of the cars produced were from the first generation, built from 2003-2008. Although some improvements (eg to the starter motor or ECU) were made along the way, the biggest changes came with the second-generation cars introduced for the 2009 model year. These can be recognised by their revised front and rear designs and optional 19in alloy wheels. More importantly, they also had changes to improve handling and increase torsional rigidity, as well as a lower final drive ratio for

First-generation RX-8, here with optional Sport styling pack. (Courtesy Mazda)

better acceleration. High Power versions received a new six-speed manual transmission from the latest MX-5. New convenience features included a more modern audio system with Bluetooth and auxiliary connections, as well as – at last! – easier access to the dipstick. The R3 – with its stiffened suspension and grippy Recaro seats – is considered by many enthusiasts to be the ultimate RX-8.

2009 R3 with revised front end and 19-inch alloys. (Courtesy Mazda)

Which engine?

All RX-8s had the same basic engine, with two 654cc rotors, giving a nominal capacity of 1308cc, so you won't be winning any barroom bragging contests! In the UK, two variants of the Renesis unit were offered from launch:
– A Standard Power version (often referred to as the 190), with four intake ports, mated to a five-speed manual transmission, developing 189bhp;
– A High Power or 230 version, with six intake ports, married to a six-speed manual, producing 228bhp.

Second-generation rotor housing (here painted grey) with third injector nozzle.

The 230 is often preferred for its revvier nature and superior (six-speed) gearbox, but the 190 should not be overlooked. Its greater torque can make it an easier drive in everyday conditions, whilst some specialists feel it is a better base if you plan to add a supercharger.

For the launch in North America, the more powerful, six-port engine was teamed with the six-speed manual transmission, whilst the less powerful four-port variant was offered with automatic transmission. Later automatics were upgraded to the six-port engine and received a boost in power to 212hp (US).

The second-generation R3 came only with the more powerful engine. The later cars are generally considered more reliable, with the addition of a third injector nozzle improving lubrication of the rotor apex seals.

Which transmission?

The high-revving characteristics of the rotary engine make it a natural match for a slick-shifting manual transmission, and the RX-8's gearbox and light clutch do not disappoint. Some customers, however, insisted on having an automatic: these were generally available in North America and imported specially into the UK by TW White & Sons in Surrey. The rotary engine's lack of low-down torque is badly suited to an automatic 'box, especially the original four-speed transmission with its widely spaced ratios. This was replaced in October 2006 by a six-speed automatic with paddle shifters, but even then it is far from an ideal combination.

Selector for optional automatic transmission. (Courtesy Mazda)

Trim levels

With the oldest cars now well past their tenth birthday, condition is likely to be more important than exact trim combinations. In the UK, the 230 versions were fitted as standard with xenon headlamps and aluminium pedals. Many cars came with leather upholstery, whilst a retractable satnav and electric sunroof were available as extras. In North America, some of these options were combined into Sport, Touring and Grand Touring packages.

Special editions

Mazda is a past master at producing limited editions to boost interest in its cars, and the RX-8 is no exception. Some of these, like the Evolve, Kuro and Nemesis in the UK, are largely cosmetic, with specific colours and leather or alcantara trim.

However, four models, all based on the first-generation cars, are worth looking out for:
– In the UK, the PZ was introduced in 2006 with input from Prodrive. It featured upgraded coil springs and dampers, unique 18in OZ alloy wheels and a Scorpion silencer. Available in Brilliant Black or Galaxy Grey, it can be also identified by its rear spoiler and Mazdaspeed door mirrors;
– The 40th Anniversary edition was launched in 2007, forty years after the original Cosmo 110S. Available in Metropolitan Grey or Crystal White, many of the changes were cosmetic, but the cars also featured specific Bilstein dampers and a polyurethane-filled front crossmember to reduce road noise;
– In the USA, Mazda produced two series of Mazdaspeed cars in 2004, featuring extra power, lowered suspension and a unique bodykit;
– Also in the USA, the Shinka was finished in Black Cherry Red Mica and equipped with performance-tuned suspension and a foam-injected front crossmember.

UK-market PZ. (Courtesy Mazda)

40th Anniversary model with Cosmo 110S behind it. (Courtesy Mazda)

Striking bodykit on US Mazdaspeed edition. (Courtesy Mazda)

5 Before you view

– be well informed

To avoid a wasted journey, and the disappointment of finding that the car does not match your expectations, it will help if you're very clear about what questions you want to ask before you pick up the telephone. Some of these points might appear basic but when you're excited about the prospect of buying your dream car, it's amazing how some of the most obvious things slip the mind ... Also check the current values of the model you are interested in on performance car websites, and look for recent auction results.

Where is the car?
Is it going to be worth travelling to the next county/state, or even across a border? A locally advertised car, although it may not sound very interesting, can add to your knowledge for very little effort, so make a visit – it might even be in better condition than expected.

Dealer or private sale
Establish early on if the car is being sold by its owner or by a trader. A private owner should have all the history, so don't be afraid to ask detailed questions. A dealer may have more limited knowledge of a car's history, but should have some documentation. A dealer may offer a warranty/guarantee (ask for a printed copy) and finance. If maintenance has been carried out in the Mazda network, you can check Mazda's Digital Service Record for the car (from 2005 in the UK, dates may vary in other markets).

Cost of collection and delivery
A dealer may well be used to quoting for delivery by car transporter. A private owner may agree to meet you halfway, but only agree to this after you have seen the car at the vendor's address to validate the documents. Conversely, you could meet halfway and agree the sale but insist on meeting at the vendor's address for the handover.

View – when and where
It is always preferable to view at the vendor's home or business premises. In the

case of a private sale, the car's documentation should tally with the vendor's name and address. Arrange to view only in daylight and avoid a wet day. Most cars look better in poor light or when wet.

When buying privately, view the car at the owner's home, even if it's not as grand as this! (Courtesy Mazda)

Reason for sale

Do make it one of the first questions. Why is the car being sold and how long has it been with the current owner? How many previous owners?

Personal imports from Japan

You may find a few JDM (Japanese Domestic Market) cars in the UK or Ireland, but steer clear of any which have the basic brakes and suspension and 16-inch wheels, which don't do justice to the cars' performance. At the other extreme, the Spirit R was a run-out special edition, which can be recognised by its 19-inch bronze alloy wheels. All cars with automatic transmission in the UK will have been specially imported, so check the import paperwork carefully. Quoted power outputs may differ from cars sold new in Europe and North America.

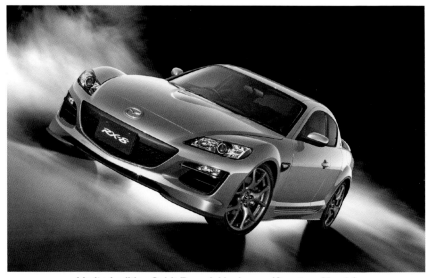

Limited edition Spirit R model in Japan. (Courtesy Mazda)

Condition (body/chassis/interior/mechanicals)

Query the car's condition in as specific terms as possible – preferably citing the checklist items described in Chapter 9.

All original specification

There is an increasing number of cars which have been customised, often for use on track. Some modified parts (such as those from Mazdaspeed) are of high quality, but if you have any doubts, steer clear. An original equipment car will often hold its value better and be easier to re-sell.

Matching data/legal ownership

Do VIN/chassis, engine numbers and licence plate match the official registration document? Is the owner's name and address recorded in the official registration documents?

For those countries that require an annual test of roadworthiness, does the car have a document showing it complies (an MoT certificate in the UK, which can be verified on 0845 600 5977)?

If a smog/emissions certificate is mandatory, does the car have one?

If required, does the car carry a current road fund licence/licence plate tag?

Does the vendor own the car outright? Money might be owed to a finance company or bank: the car could even be stolen. Several organisations will supply the data on ownership, based on the car's licence plate number, for a fee. Such companies can often also tell you whether the car has been 'written-off' by an insurance company. In the UK, these organisations can supply vehicle data:

HPI	01722 422 422
AA	0870 600 0836
DVLA	0870 240 0010
RAC	0870 533 3660

Other countries will have similar organisations.

Insurance
Check with your existing insurer before setting out, your current policy might not cover you to drive the car if you do purchase it.

How you can pay
A cheque/check will take several days to clear and the seller may prefer to sell to a cash buyer. However, a banker's draft (a cheque issued by a bank) is as good as cash, but safer, so contact your own bank and become familiar with the formalities that are necessary to obtain one.

Buying at auction?
If your intention is to buy at auction, see Chapter 10 for further advice.

Professional vehicle check (vehicle examination)
There are often marque/model specialists who will undertake professional examination of a vehicle on your behalf. Owners' clubs will be able to put you in touch with such specialists.

Other organisations that will carry out a general professional check in the UK are:

AA	0800 085 3007 (motoring organisation with vehicle inspectors)
ABS	0800 358 5855 (specialist vehicle inspection company)
RAC	0870 533 3660 (motoring organisation with vehicle inspectors)

Other countries will have similar organisations.

www.velocebooks.com / www.veloce.co.uk
Details of all current books • New book news • Special offers • Gift vouchers • Forum

17

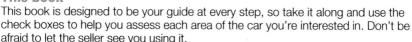
This book
This book is designed to be your guide at every step, so take it along and use the check boxes to help you assess each area of the car you're interested in. Don't be afraid to let the seller see you using it.

Reading glasses (if you need them for close work)
Take your reading glasses if you need them to read documents and make close up inspections.

Ask the seller to remove the engine cover for a closer look.

Torch
A torch with fresh batteries will be useful for peering into the wheelarches and under the car.

Magnet (not powerful, a fridge magnet is ideal)
A magnet will help you check if the car is full of filler, or has fibreglass panels. Use the magnet to sample bodywork areas all around the car, but be careful not to damage the paintwork. Expect to find a little filler here and there, but not whole panels.

Probe (a small screwdriver works very well)
A small screwdriver can be used – with care – as a probe, particularly in the wheelarches and on the underside. With this you should be able to check an area

of severe corrosion, but be careful – if it's really bad, the screwdriver might go right through the metal!

Overalls
Be prepared to get dirty. Take along a pair of overalls, if you have them.

Mirror on a stick
Fixing a mirror at an angle on the end of a stick may seem odd, but you'll probably need it to check the condition of the underside of the car. It will also

This wheelarch definitely needs investigation.

help you to peer into some of the important crevices. You can also use it, together with the torch, along the underside of the sills and on the floor.

Digital camera (or smartphone)
If you have a digital camera or smartphone, take it along so that, later, you can study some areas of the car more closely. Take a picture of any part of the car that causes you concern, and seek a friend's opinion. Like the mirror on a stick, a 'selfie stick' may help you get your smartphone under the car.

A friend, preferably a knowledgeable enthusiast
Ideally, have a friend or knowledgeable enthusiast accompany you: a second opinion is always valuable.

7 Fifteen-minute evaluation
– walk away or stay?

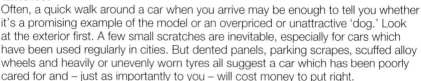

Exterior
Often, a quick walk around a car when you arrive may be enough to tell you whether it's a promising example of the model or an overpriced or unattractive 'dog.' Look at the exterior first. A few small scratches are inevitable, especially for cars which have been used regularly in cities. But dented panels, parking scrapes, scuffed alloy wheels and heavily or unevenly worn tyres all suggest a car which has been poorly cared for and – just as importantly to you – will cost money to put right.

Look carefully along the line of the car on each side for dents or uneven panels, then step back from it to check for mismatched paint on different panels, which may be the result of poor accident repairs.

Parking scrapes can be costly to repair.

This sorry-looking wheel needs complete refurbishment.

Light seats like this show up wear and discolouration.

Interior and boot (trunk)
Inside, dirty seats and scratched or damaged trim tell the same story. There are plenty of good RX-8s out there, so be ready to move on.

Open the luggage compartment too: is the tyre repair kit present and correct? Don't be put off by the sight of a spare bottle of oil, which is often the sign of a caring owner.

The engine compartment
Take a look at the engine compartment: it needn't be immaculately clean (in fact, that may be suspicious on a ten-year old car), but it should be free from obvious leaks, damaged hoses and trailing wires.

Tyre repair kit and spare oil.

A bit dusty, but otherwise this engine looks okay.

Before the test drive

If the car seems promising after that first look, resist the temptation to get behind the wheel and go straight for a test drive. There's a lot more you can check very quickly on the dealer's forecourt or a private seller's driveway.

Which model is it?

The first thing to confirm is exactly which model you are looking at. Is the car you are viewing as described? Is it the Standard or High Power version, for example? Which transmission does it have? When was it built (which may be well before the date of first registration)? These questions seem obvious, yet it is amazing how many vendors – whether negligent private sellers or traders unfamiliar with the RX-8 – provide inaccurate information about the car for sale.

PZ-style mirror, but this red car is no PZ.

If you are considering one of the limited edition models, is it genuine? Is all the special equipment present and correct? Be wary of standard cars which may just have one or two trim parts added, such as the door mirrors or rear spoiler from a PZ, but without the uprated suspension.

Modifications

There is a long tradition of modifying Japanese performance cars, and in the USA especially you will find many RX-8s that have been modified. However, its unique rotary powerplant makes this a more complicated undertaking than for piston-engined cars. Remapping the ECU has been known to cause problems, and you should steer clear of any 'flex fuel' kits which claim to let the car run on E85 (bioethanol).

Forced induction – whether a turbo kit or Pettit Racing's supercharger – seems like a natural choice for the RX-8, boosting its limited torque, but the increase in power and resulting higher exhaust gas temperatures can exacerbate wear of the side seals on the rotors and shorten the life of the engine.

If you are still willing to consider a modified car, look for high-quality parts from reputable suppliers, like a Scorpion exhaust (as fitted to the PZ) or the lightened flywheel and quickshift kit from Mazdaspeed. Make sure, too, that the parts were installed by a rotary specialist, to minimise the risk of problems later on.

Sticker from a well-known RX-8 tuner: check what modifications have been done!

Is it genuine and legal?

However attractive the car may look at first, it's essential that the paperwork is in order. First of all, does the VIN (the 17-digit Vehicle Identification Number) on the car tally with that on the registration/title document? On the RX-8, you can find this on a plate attached to the right-hand side of the bulkhead in the engine compartment. Make sure that the ID plate hasn't gone missing or been tampered with. Take a note or photograph of the VIN for reference: you can look it up online later to confirm the year of manufacture of the car or check its service history in the Mazda dealer network. Independent organisations (see Chapter 5) will also let you check that there is no finance outstanding on the car and no record of serious accident damage. If something doesn't seem right here, walk away now. At best, you may have problems registering the car; at worst, it may be stolen or unroadworthy.

Does the seller's name and address appear on the registration or title document? How many owners has the car had? Frequent changes of ownership, especially recently, often point to serious problems which cash-strapped owners haven't had the budget to put right. If you are buying privately, be sure to view the car at the owner's home address, so that you can check this tallies with the paperwork for the car.

If all these details are correct, ask to see evidence of the car's service history including, if possible, invoices for work done, showing the parts which have been replaced. Don't be put off by work carried out by independent rotary specialists rather than by Mazda dealers; on the contrary, many of these independents now

ID plate with the all-important VIN.

have the best knowledge of the RX-8. If the car requires an annual roadworthiness certificate in your country (such as the MoT test in the UK), make sure that this is current, and note any advisories, indicating work that should be done. You may be able to use these to negotiate a reduction in the price you pay. Finally, make sure that the mileage on the car's odometer matches that on the service documentation or test certificates.

Ask the seller

Even if you are well used to buying secondhand cars, it's hard to spot all the potential faults in just a few minutes. Often, you can learn just as much, if not more, in the first few minutes by putting some questions to the seller.

How has the seller used the car? As with any high-performance car, track use can be hard on tyres, suspension and brakes, and rotaries don't like lots of short journeys in town.

How has the car been maintained? Ideally, at an independent RX-8 specialist or an official Mazda dealership with plenty of rotary experience. When were important service items like the coil packs or plugs last replaced? Were OEM or high-quality replacement parts used? What service recalls – to upgrade the starter motor, for example – have been carried out? You can access complete lists of these through the owners' forums online or, armed with the VIN, from an official Mazda dealer. There were a good many recalls and TSBs (technical service bulletins) for first-generation cars, so most of them should have been carried out by now; by the time the second-generation models were introduced, many of these service issues had been fixed.

Does the car suffer from any hot starting problems? As we will see in Chapter 9, this is the acid test for every RX-8 as it gets older, and something you should check for yourself on a test drive. If the seller seems evasive or tries to minimise this issue, be very wary indeed. At one leading RX-8 specialist in France, all four cars recently awaiting engine rebuilds were the subject of legal disputes with their sellers. Buyer beware indeed!

A genuine and enthusiastic seller, on the other hand, can do a lot to put you at ease. If the vendor is a member of one of the owners' clubs or online groups, that usually means that he (or she) takes an active interest in looking after the car and is aware of its foibles.

Road test

If this is your first drive in an RX-8, this will be a moment you've long been looking forward to. In the excitement to get going, make sure that the insurance on the car covers you to drive it.

If the engine is cold, the owner may be concerned that you will stall the engine and immediately re-start it, perhaps when manoeuvring the car out of its parking place; he may even want to drive it first himself. Don't be put off by this: it's almost certainly a positive sign that the vendor knows the risks of flooding the engine when it's cold and the problems which can ensue. Watching the owner drive a car can often be very informative: does he (or she) ride the clutch or rev the engine hard while it's still cold, for instance?

If, on the other hand, the engine is already warm, be sure to check that it starts promptly. If it was cold when you started your test drive, make sure that the test drive is long enough for it to come fully up to temperature, and try re-starting it when you return to base. Whenever starting the engine, look for any blue smoke coming from the exhaust. A little steam when the engine is cold, however, is normal, as water burns off the exhaust system.

If the engine starts as it should, you can concentrate on enjoying your test drive and assessing the RX-8 as you would any other car. Keep the radio off (you

The road test will tell you a lot about the car. (Courtesy Mazda)

can test that when the car is parked up later) and drop the driver's window, so that you can hear any rattles or untoward noises from the engine or exhaust system. Let the engine come up to temperature before revving it hard; the final cars had a progressively shaded rev counter, with the red line gradually increasing as the engine warms through.

Try and drive the car on a variety of roads, including some out-of-town stretches where you can open up the engine. The smoothness of the RX-8's engine is legendary, so it should rev freely and without vibration all the way to the red line. Work your way through the gears, making sure that the clutch operates smoothly and that each gear engages cleanly. On the 5-speed manual gearbox, the shift from second to third gear can sometimes be slightly notchy; on the 6-speed 'box, fourth can be a little slow to engage. Otherwise, the gearshift action should be quick and positive. If the clutch is slipping or has a high biting point, it's probably on its way

Corroded or warped discs can cause brake judder.

out, so you will need to budget for a replacement. On cars fitted with automatic transmission, check the transmission operates correctly in both automatic and manual modes.

Try and find a clear stretch of open road, where you can take your hands off the wheel: the car should continue to run straight. If it doesn't, closer examination and an alignment check will be required. The RX-8 is a great-handling car, and the steering should seem light and precise, without excessive free play.

Apply the brakes a few times: they should operate smoothly. Any judder usually means that the discs are warped or corroded, an expensive item to replace. When there is nobody behind you – and after warning the seller first! – try making an emergency stop: the car should pull up straight, without veering to either side. With sufficient pressure, and particularly if the road is wet or greasy, you should feel the anti-lock braking system (ABS) kick in as the brake pedal pulses under your foot. Any failings here will need further investigation.

Not a runner?
What if the car can't be driven at all? If the rest of the car presents well, and the price is low enough, it may still be worth considering as the basis for restoration (with a new or rebuilt engine) or as a parts car.

www.velocebooks.com / www.veloce.co.uk
Details of all current books • New book news • Special offers • Gift vouchers • Forum

24

8 Key points
– where to look for problems

'Location, location, location ...' the estate agents say. For would-be RX-8 owners, everything comes down to 'Engine, engine, engine ...'

Engine and mechanicals

The RX-8's unique rotary engine is the heart of the car, and the health of the engine is the key to a successful purchase. Rotary engines will fail, often after 60,000 miles (100,000km) or so, although much depends on how they have been driven and maintained. Problems starting a hot engine and blue smoke from the exhaust are among the danger signs, warning that an expensive engine rebuild or replacement is looming.

Otherwise, the transmission, brakes and suspension present few major problems, though watch for corrosion on the front subframe.

The heart of the matter. (Courtesy Mazda)

Once removed from the car, the state of this subframe can be seen.

Bodywork and interior

Despite its unusual design, the bodyshell of the RX-8 is highly rigid. Significant corrosion is rare, but check the rear wheelarches, including the leading edge, especially on cars fitted with body kits. Inspect personal imports from Japan with particular care, as these may not have been adequately rustproofed from new.

Inside, the RX-8 is well assembled and should be durable. Some of the electrical accessories can cause problems, so make sure everything works as intended.

Here, rust has set in underneath a plastic sill panel.

Check that all the electrics work, including the audio system.

9 Serious evaluation

– 60 minutes for years of enjoyment

Circle the Excellent, Good, Average or Poor box of each section as you go along. The totting up procedure is detailed at the end of the chapter. Be realistic in your marking!

If you've come this far, congratulations! The paperwork is in order and the car looks promising. Now is the time to take a really thorough look at your intended purchase, bearing in mind the points already mentioned in the last two chapters. Try and be systematic in your examination of the car, so that you don't miss anything. Start with a close look at the bodywork and exterior of the car, before turning your attention to the interior and finally the engine and underbody.

Exterior

First impressions

Make sure that you can view the car outdoors and in daylight, preferably in good weather. The car should be clean; it's hard to judge the appearance of paintwork under a layer of dirt or road grime!

Begin by stepping back from the car and noting how it sits on the road. Does it appear to sag on either side or at one end? That could be the result of a problem with the suspension. Some owners may have lowered the suspension: do the wheels still clear the wheelarches? Will the front spoiler (especially if the car has a Mazdaspeed or other aftermarket bodykit) ground on speed bumps? Run your hand along the underside of the front spoiler to check for existing damage to the paintwork.

Take special care if the car you are looking at has been used on track: the RX-8's bodyshell is very rigid, but circuit use puts exceptional demands on any car. A roll cage gives extra protection to the driver, but also strengthens the whole body.

Ground clearance is reduced on this car with a Mazdaspeed bodykit.
(Courtesy Mazda)

Bodywork

Look at the overall condition of the body: are the panels straight and crease-free, without any serious dents? Crouch down and look along the side of the car, to see if anything seems out of line.

Like so many modern cars, the RX-8's bodywork – especially its flared wheelarches and side sills – is very exposed to scratches and 'dings' in everyday use. Rear parking sensors were never fitted as standard (although they were available as dealer-fit accessories), so the rear bumper (fender) is particularly vulnerable. If the front or rear bumper has been scraped, is the panel itself still solidly attached to the car and free from cracks?

Do all the panels look straight?

Aluminium body panels

To save weight, some body panels, including the rear doors, boot (trunk) lid and bonnet (hood), are made from aluminium. The bonnet has only a simple manual prop to hold it open. Make sure it hasn't been damaged when it has been closed or if any items have been placed on it. Does it open and close cleanly? Not all body shops can handle aluminium, so if any of these panels show signs of having been repaired, check how well the work has been done.

Rear doors are made from aluminium. (Courtesy Mazda)

Oil radiators

While you are at the front of the car, look at the apertures for the oil radiators at each side of the car. Mazda didn't fit any kind of protection, leaving them very exposed. Are they free from leaves or other debris? Do the radiators themselves appear to be in good condition? If they are blocked, you can use an airline to clear out any muck, but the best long-term solution is to fit an accessory mesh grille over them.

Aftermarket mesh grille provides effective protection to the oil radiator.

Doors

Pay special attention to the so-called 'Freestyle' doors, which should be perfectly aligned, with even gaps around them. If that isn't the case, the car may have suffered a side impact which hasn't been properly repaired. The side doors are also liable to minor damage due to their unconventional design: passengers unfamiliar with the car may try to close the rear door after the front one. In narrow parking spaces it can be hard to get out of the car, with the result that bags or belts can scratch the paintwork.

While looking at the doors, examine the condition of the rubber door seals, to make sure they are not perished or otherwise damaged, especially on cars built

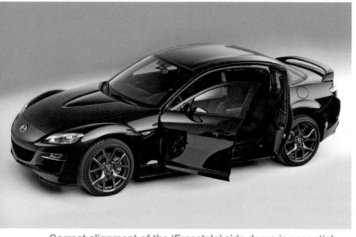

Correct alignment of the 'Freestyle' side doors is essential.
(Courtesy Mazda)

Side door seals should be in good condition, as here.

Front door can be damaged if closed incorrectly.

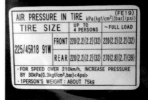

Tyre information sticker should be present inside the driver's door.

before 2006 (when Mazda changed their design). Make sure that the sticker on the driver's side opening which specifies the tyre size and pressures is present: replacing it is a detail which is sometimes overlooked when accident repairs are carried out.

Paintwork ④ ③ ② ①

Most RX-8s were delivered in a range of metallic 'Mica' finishes. The manufacturer used Velocity Red Mica on many of its launch cars, and it became the 'signature' colour for the car. You can check the paint code on the sticker inside the driver's door.

Whichever colour you choose, make sure that the paint appears even and consistent across all the panels. A difference in shade between adjacent steel panels may suggest that the car has been repainted after an accident. A slight difference between the plastic front or rear bumpers and the neighbouring steel panels is perfectly normal though, and nothing to be concerned about. The nose section is most exposed to stone chips, so a repainted front panel may even be a sign of a meticulous owner who has taken good care of the car. You will find

Front panel may suffer from stone chips. (Courtesy Mazda)

more guidance on assessing paintwork condition in Chapter 14, but there are few paintwork problems specific to the RX-8.

Some cars have been fitted with stick-on front number plates, intended to improve the car's appearance. They are, however, illegal in some countries, including the UK, and the adhesive used may damage the paintwork when you come to remove it.

Body corrosion

Outside Japan, the RX-8 was sold with a generous warranty against corrosion breakthrough (12 years in the UK, for example), and major corrosion to the exterior of the car is rare. You should pay particular attention to the wheelarches: look for signs of paint bubbling on the surface and run your hand around the inside of the arch. Does it feel solid? The leading edge of the rear wheelarches is also prone to corrosion and may be partly hidden from view if the car has been fitted with a bodykit. Be ready to get down on the ground to examine them closely. A small magnet will help you detect the presence of filler.

Removing the wheel may make it easier to see rust around the rear wheelarches.

Wheel hubs and brake callipers may need repainting. (Courtesy Mazda)

You may find minor rust spots on the inner door sills, if the rubber door seal has failed in the middle, and around the high-level brakelight on the boot lid.

When the car was new, Mazda came in for a lot of criticism for the poor finish of the wheel hubs and brake callipers, which showed signs of surface corrosion after only a few months. Many dealers repainted these parts under warranty, but if it hasn't been done, it's an easy job for a home mechanic.

Wheels

A car's wheels can tell you a lot about how the car has been cared for by its last owner. Minor damage from kerbing can be made good by wheel refurbishment specialists. More serious damage, however, may affect the car's handling. If one

Badly damaged wheel from first-generation car.

of the alloy wheels is damaged and the car pulls to one side, ask to get the alignment checked. The RX-8 is no worse than many cars of its age, but significant corrosion to the wheels should also cause alarm bells to ring. If the wheels have suffered damage from salt on winter roads, what about the rest of the car? You might be able to negotiate a reduced price to cover the cost of a new or refurbished set of alloys, but corrosion damage to the subframes or other underbody components is potentially serious. If you have any doubts, try to inspect the car on a ramp.

Chrome and other trim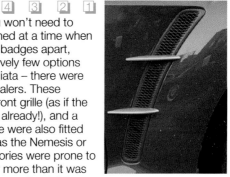

Pitted or rusty chrome is one thing you won't need to worry about on the RX-8. It was designed at a time when chrome was out of fashion, and, shiny badges apart, its trim is all black. Mazda offered relatively few options on the RX-8, but – as with the MX-5/Miata – there were plenty of accessories available from dealers. These included a rotary crest for the central front grille (as if the car didn't have enough rotor emblems already!), and a set of strakes for the side grilles. (These were also fitted to some special edition models, such as the Nemesis or Evolve.) Early versions of these accessories were prone to surface corrosion, which was unsightly more than it was serious; Mazda later switched to higher-quality stainless steel.

Accessory side strakes can corrode.

Glass and sunroof

Examine the windscreen, side windows and rear screen in turn. If any of the windows have been tinted, is the depth of tint within the legally allowable limits in your country? Is the film used in good condition, or showing signs of cracks or lifting off?

The condition of the windscreen is especially important, as it is most likely to be damaged by stone chips. A crack in the driver's line of sight may cause the car to fail a roadworthiness inspection.

If the car you are looking at has a sunroof, ensure that the mechanism is well greased, and that it opens and closes smoothly. The drainage channels should be clear. A rattling sunroof, however, needn't be a cause for concern: it can be easily fixed with an adjustment to the sunshade, and a differently-shaped pin mechanism.

Rattling front windows, too, can be readily sorted, by lowering them by 1mm.

Check optional sunroof for operation and leaks. (Courtesy Mazda)

Interior
Upholstery

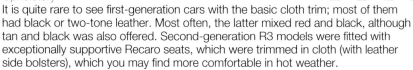

It is quite rare to see first-generation cars with the basic cloth trim; most of them had black or two-tone leather. Most often, the latter mixed red and black, although tan and black was also offered. Second-generation R3 models were fitted with exceptionally supportive Recaro seats, which were trimmed in cloth (with leather side bolsters), which you may find more comfortable in hot weather.

Some of the special edition models were trimmed in a lighter colour, referred to as 'Stone' or 'Parchment': leather on the Nemesis and Shinka, and a mix of leather and alcantara on the Evolve and 40th Anniversary models. Like any light trim, this picks up dirt easily; the alcantara material can soon look especially grubby and prove difficult to revive.

Most cars came with leather seats. (Courtesy Mazda)

Cloth-trimmed seats from Recaro are ideal in hard cornering. (Courtesy Mazda)

Lighter leather and alcantara wear less well.

Fixtures and fittings

A few owners have complained of rattles from the doors and interior trim, but in general the interior is well screwed together. Although Mazda used real aluminium for the pedals and the rotor emblem in the front head restraints, it doesn't have the quality feel of German rivals like the Audi TT, and the carpet is notably thin. The hard plastics used are certainly durable, but scratch easily: look for signs of wear on the kick plates, the silver trim strips along the edges of the transmission tunnel and, on pre-2006 cars, the casings for the front seats. The sides of the front seats can also be damaged by seatbelt buckles, whilst the driver's seat bolsters are particularly liable to wear. You may find damage to the climate control buttons, the sun visors, and the cover over the storage compartment between the rear seats, so inspect these carefully.

While you are looking around the front seats, check the gaiter of the handbrake (parking brake), as the rubber casing can break off, leaving an unsightly hole. If the car you are viewing was fitted with an illuminated gear knob as an accessory, check that the lighting is still working, as the part is no longer available new.

Look up too at the headlining, to check for any tears or discolouration.

Check sun visors for cracks; perforations are by design!

Door sills and silver trim on the transmission tunnel and seat casings all scratch easily. (Courtesy Mazda)

Trim around handbrake can be damaged. (Courtesy Mazda)

Boot (trunk)

4 3 2 1

Don't forget to look inside the luggage compartment. You should be able to open the boot from outside the car, by using the remote control lever under the dashboard or with the remote central locking key. The car should come complete with its tyre repair kit and, very likely, a spare bottle of oil. If the bottle is not tightly closed, it's all too easy for oil to leak out, quickly impregnating the thin carpet, so check the condition of that as well.

Is the carpet clean and undamaged?

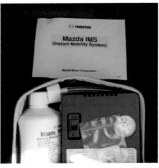

Tyre repair kit should contain compressor and sealant.

Electrics

Now is a good time to check the operation of the different items of electrical equipment on the car. If you find that something isn't working as it should, it may be nothing more than a blown bulb or faulty fuse. You'll find the fuses under a panel next to the pedals inside the car and adjacent to the battery and air filter in the engine compartment; the owner's manual lists the function covered by each fuse. Anything more than this, however, may signal an expensive repair, or risk the car failing a safety inspection such as the MoT in the UK. The only sure way here is to work your way round the car, methodically testing each of the controls in turn. The RX-8 has a few known trouble spots, so take particular care checking these.

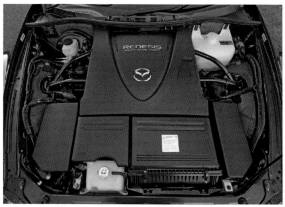

Fuses are under the plastic panels at the front to the right of the battery. (Courtesy Mazda)

Audio system

Make sure that the CD player (if fitted) works correctly. The audio system is a modular one, with an interchangeable unit which – depending on model specification and year of production – might be a cassette deck, a single or multi-CD player or even a MiniDisc (MD) module. If only the CD player has failed, you may be able to find a used replacement module. Later CD players were MP3-compatible, whilst second-generation cars added an auxiliary jack (under the front centre armrest) and Bluetooth connectivity for mobile phones.

Second-generation audio system with six CD changer.

Listen to the AM/FM radio with the heated rear windscreen switched on. If the reception suffers from interference, the only solution is to fit an unsightly external aerial (antenna) … or switch off the radio! The first three wires act as an antenna, so don't be surprised if they don't seem to have any effect demisting the screen!

Radio display at the top of the dash. (Courtesy Mazda)

Satellite navigation

One more feature was much appreciated back in the day, but is now a very mixed blessing: the satellite navigation (or GPS) system, fitted as standard to higher-spec cars or as an option. There have been reports of this failing to close down correctly, leading to severe battery drain, which can

Satnav system has aged badly. (Courtesy Mazda)

flatten the battery completely in less than two days. As if starting an RX-8 wasn't challenging enough already! Even if the satnav unit is working correctly, the software is now very outdated and map updates are no longer available. You'll be better off using an aftermarket satnav or a routing app on your smartphone.

Other equipment

If you are testing the car in a very hot or humid climate, the air-conditioning may seem weak. If it is working, albeit feebly, it may be, as with any used car, that the system merely needs recharging. Even when it has been regularly maintained though, it still isn't the RX-8's best feature.

Cars fitted with the accessory reversing sensors (or 'park assist') sometimes beep unnecessarily, but this fault is probably best ignored.

Air-conditioning isn't very powerful, but should still be working.

Dealer-fit rear parking sensors can give false alerts.

Lighting

If the car you are viewing is fitted with the desirable xenon (HID) headlamps, check that the levelling sensors work correctly, as these are expensive to replace. (Halogen lights are manually adjusted.) Try the headlamp washers. With the ignition and headlamps on, pull the windscreen wiper lever quickly towards you twice. If the headlamp washers don't work, it may simply be that the fluid level is low. If there is too little fluid left in the reservoir, the car's system gives preference to the windscreen washers. A smart feature, but which can be disconcerting at first!

Are any of the lights damaged in any way? That could mean a fail during a safety inspection and an unavoidable repair bill.

Finishing your inspection at the rear of the car, look for condensation or moisture inside the lights. The seals on the lights sometimes fail, which may allow water into the luggage compartment. On later cars, this fault was fixed by Mazda.

Xenon headlamps with washer unit below.

Rear light units can let in moisture.

Battery

After checking all the controls from inside the car, open the bonnet and lift the plastic cover over the battery. The original battery fitted to the first cars was weak, causing starting problems. Most RX-8s on sale today will be on their second or third replacement battery, so it should be up to the job. Some owners may have been tempted to fit a physically larger battery; make sure that the dimensions are correct for the car, and that the battery compartment is properly

Unclip the cover to inspect the battery.

ventilated. On older cars especially, look for signs of corrosion around the battery resulting from leaks. If not treated promptly, rust here can soon spread.

Engine and mechanicals

Enthusiasts with long memories won't need reminding that the rotary engine's reliability has always been its Achilles heel. Early long-term reports in the motoring press praised the lack of problems with the RX-8's rotary engine and the cars' typically Japanese reliability. With no cambelt to change and only three main moving parts to worry about, the rotary apparently had a lot going for it.

Nowadays, many RX-8 owners will paint a very different picture. So what went wrong? Unless you strip down a rotary engine on the workbench, many of the issues with worn components cannot easily be seen. It's all the more important therefore to watch for those faults which are symptomatic of serious engine problems.

Some workshops will say that these problems usually occur after 60,000 miles (100,000km), but it is hard to be categorical. A new engine may be required after

You can quickly remove the top cover to inspect the engine.

The rotor inside the combustion chamber. (Courtesy Mazda)

just 25,000 miles (40,000km), but you may also find a car still running sweetly on its first engine at 150,000 miles (240,000km). Everything depends on how the car has been driven and maintained. Plenty of motorway/freeway use and regular bursts of higher revs when the engine is warm (taking care not to hit the rev limiter too often) will help prevent carbon deposits building up in the engine. Short city journeys, on the other hand, when the engine rarely gets the chance to warm up or run at higher speeds, do it no favours at all.

As a buyer, you should ask for copies of bills or other documentation to prove that servicing work has been done, as well as performing the checks suggested below yourself.

Apex seals 　　④ ③ ② ①

When Mazda launched the RX-8, it set a target of 150,000 miles (240,000km) before the rotors' apex seals would need to be replaced and the engine rebuilt. If the engine is difficult to start when hot, this could be due to problems with the coils and plugs, so ask the seller when they were last replaced. More often than not, however, this will be a sign of low compression resulting from apex seal wear. Over time, uneven wear to the apex seals is almost inevitable, due to the way in which they are lubricated. If the car appears to be down on power, or the seller admits that the fuel consumption has increased, that will confirm that diagnosis. The only solution is to replace or rebuild the engine.

Well-worn rotor housing on the workbench.

Look in the rear-view mirror or from behind the car for signs of blue smoke from the exhaust. This is caused by a worn 'O' ring or seals on the rotor housing, and again a new or rebuilt engine will be needed.

Watch for blue smoke from the exhaust!

Stationary gear bearings 　　④ ③ ② ①

Although the apex seal issues are well known, some specialists in fact consider failure of the stationary gear bearings (which worsens over time) to be the primary cause of engine failure on the RX-8. This problem is caused by extremely low oil pressure in the Renesis engine at idle and is inherent in its design. These are the warning signs to listen out for:

• A low droning noise from the engine, from idle upwards;
• A rattling sound from the engine at high revs (the engine may also be reluctant to rev);
• A sharp, loud clatter at start-up, especially after the car has been left standing for some time.

Serious wear is evident inside this bearing.

The only solution to this problem is, you guessed it ... to replace or rebuild the engine completely.

If either problem is present, it is essential to go into the purchase of an RX-8 with your eyes open ... and your cheque book safely tucked away. If the price is low enough, buying an otherwise solid car which needs a new engine doesn't have to be a 'no-no,' but unscrupulous sellers may try to play down some of these issues, leaving you with unexpected problems and big bills. You will find more advice on rebuilding or replacing the engine in Chapter 13.

Oil & fuel   4 3 2 1

Given the importance of oil to lubricate the rotors, it may seem obvious to state that the oil level should be checked regularly (at least once every 1000 miles/1600km) and kept topped up. Mazda hardly helped owners, as the dipstick and oil filler cap are hidden under a plastic panel. Second-generation cars were better designed, with a separate, small cover for the dipstick, but adding oil still means removing the plastic engine cover. Be sure to check the level yourself, after the engine has run for at least five minutes. If the low oil light on the dash is already on, it's a bad sign. It may, however, flash briefly under very hard cornering or from 4500-4800rpm, which is not a cause for concern. On second-generation cars, Mazda re-designed the oil pan, effectively overcoming this problem.

Mazda recommends the use of a 5W30 semi-synthetic oil, such as its own Dexelia product, developed by Elf. A visit to the online forums will quickly bring up a good deal of debate as to whether this is best, or whether a thicker 10W40 oil will provide better protection for the engine. In any event, the RX-8 engine requires semi-synthetic rather than fully synthetic oil, as the latter will leave more carbon deposits behind. Check with the seller for evidence that the oil has been changed regularly; many owners will change it more frequently than the interval of 12,500 miles (20,000km) originally recommended by Mazda in Europe.

Incidentally, if the oil on the dipstick looks milky, and seems to be foaming, that is the result of condensation and is perfectly normal. It often occurs after the car has been used for several short journeys. Mazda offered a modified dipstick and cap as a solution; it may also be possible to resolve the problem by flushing the system with a specially formulated cleaning oil.

Oil leaks are rare, but take a good look around the engine bay and under the car, especially if it has been standing for some time. Corrosion can sometimes affect the set of three oil cooler lines; this is a potentially serious fault to check, as oil could leak onto the brakes. Some dealers only replaced one of the lines during the recall campaign, so check the condition of all

At last! A separate cover for the dipstick on second-generation cars.

Fuel grade (here for Europe) is shown inside the filler cap.

three lines carefully. Stainless steel replacements are now available, and a desirable replacement for any cars you are looking over.

The RX-8 requires premium grade unleaded fuel; many owners use the highest grade available.

Ignition: coils, plugs and leads   ④ ③ ② ①

It is critical to check when the plugs, coils and leads were last replaced. The coil packs should be replaced every 30,000 miles or 50,000km, the sparkplugs and leads not later than every 37,500 miles/60,000km. Failing ignition coils aggravate wear on the engine, as unburned fuel washes away the layer of oil intended to lubricate the rotor seals. The ensuing lack of lubrication causes excessive wear to the seals, and other internal components.

The problem of flooding the engine after a cold start, which has already been described, is more than just an inconvenience, as it can cause the sparkplugs to soot-up. It is important that all the plugs are changed at the same time; one of them needs a special tool to get at, so some mechanics may be tempted to skimp on the job.

Coils and wiring should be renewed regularly.

Exhaust system   ④ ③ ② ①

The catalytic converter is the source of two potential problems with the RX-8. If you hear a rattle from the exhaust, this can signify that the catalytic converter will need to be replaced, which will mean an expensive visit to the workshop (see parts prices in Chapter 2). Fuel consumption that is even higher than usual can result from a failed lambda sensor in the catalytic converter; the associated increase in exhaust emissions will lead to the car failing mandatory inspections such as the MoT test in the UK, so repairing it is an essential job.

Catalytic converter removed for replacement.

Cooling system   ④ ③ ② ①

If the cooling warning light comes on, it may be nothing more serious than the sensor in the expansion tank activating unnecessarily. This may be due to the tank being overfilled, or the result of age-related wear in the float, which ends up triggering the warning light. In the latter

The coolant expansion tank has to be replaced as a single unit.

The temperature gauge is to the right of the instrument display. (Courtesy Mazda)

case, fixing it means replacing the entire expansion tank, as the sensor is an integral part of it. To avoid this cost, some owners unplug the sensor altogether. Which is fine, until the day you really do need that warning! Make sure therefore that you check the coolant level yourself under the bonnet.

More worrying is when the coolant level drops and the temperature rises, so keep an eye on the temperature gauge during your test drive. These symptoms may be the result of the coolant seals failing, causing coolant to leak into the combustion chambers. A professional workshop can check for this by performing a pressure test on the cooling system and examining an oil sample for contamination. If the coolant seals have failed, an engine rebuild or replacement will be called for.

Transmission
[4] [3] [2] [1]

The majority of RX-8s are fitted with manual transmissions, which have an excellent reputation. Whether the car is fitted with the five-speed or six-speed gearbox, the gears should engage quickly and positively. The change from second into third on the five-speed gearbox may be slightly notchy, although this usually improves over time; similarly, on the six-speed 'box, fourth may seem to baulk slightly.

The clutch should last from 50,000 to 80,000 miles (80,000-130,000km), although this is very dependent on how the car is driven. If the biting point seems high or you sense the clutch slipping, it will need to be replaced soon. If the gearbox rattles when in neutral, the car will need a new clutch release bearing.

For cars with automatic transmission, check during the test drive that the gears change up and down smoothly, both in fully automatic mode (does the kickdown operate as it should?) and manually, using the paddle shifters. Early cars had a four-speed automatic; from late 2006, this was replaced by a six-speed transmission.

Six-speed manual transmission has an especially good reputation. (Courtesy Mazda)

Silver paddle shifters can be seen behind the wheel on this US-market car. (Courtesy Mazda)

Suspension

Thanks to weight-saving measures like its aluminium panels and carbon-fibre propshaft, the RX-8 is reasonably light, most models coming in at under 1400kg (3000lb). As a result, it is relatively easy on its suspension and brakes. The suspension geometry is also straightforward to set up and adjust, an important consideration for track day use.

The very first cars built (until December 2003) risked developing cracks in the suspension ball joints, but all of these should have been dealt with through the manufacturer's recall programme. You should, however, still check the anti-roll bars for possible cracks, as well as the front crossmember (see section on 'Underbody' below). If you hear any knocking from the front over bumps, that may signify worn front anti-roll bar drop links, which will need to be replaced. A clicking sound from the front end on full lock was the subject of a service bulletin (TSB) to Mazda's dealer network, so that should have been attended to by now. Look for signs of leaks from the shock absorbers, which will mean they have to be replaced. The Bilstein units fitted to some models such as the UK-market PZ cost more than twice as much as the standard items.

Cutaway view of front brakes and suspension. (Courtesy Mazda)

Tyres

Take a close look at the tyres, checking for any damage to the sidewalls and for uneven tread wear, which may be the result of poor alignment. All four tyres should be of the same make and size, meeting the manufacturer's specification. You will find a sticker on the leading edge of the rear door on the driver's side, showing the recommended rating and pressures. Even if the car you are looking at has the optional tyre pressure monitoring system (TPMS), it's always a good idea to check the pressures with a handheld gauge when the tyres are cold. If you have one, use a tread depth gauge to see how much useful life the tyres still have: the legal limit in the UK, for instance, is 1.6mm, but 3mm or even 4mm is a much safer limit for a high-performance car like the RX-8. Check the DOT code on the sidewall of each tyre to confirm their date of manufacture: even if they are little used, rubber hardens after five years or so and the tyres will perform less well. If the tyres on the car you are considering will soon need to be changed, try and use that as a bargaining tool when negotiating the price.

Plenty of tread is essential on a high-performance car. (Courtesy Mazda)

Mazda originally fitted Bridgestone tyres to the RX-8: the RE040 on the first-generation cars with 18in wheels and the RE050 on later cars. Many owners, the author included, disliked the RE040, because of its poor grip in the wet, and tendency to follow ruts in the road. At the front, the Bridgestone tyres also tended to wear faster on the outside edges, leaving a narrow central contact patch; be careful if these have been recently been switched to the rear of the car, as the reduced contact area can make the car skittish when cornering hard. You will find many cars on sale now with other tyres. Popular replacement choices include the Toyo Proxes, Vredestein Ultrac Sessenta and Yokohama Advan Sport. Tyre wear is heavily dependent on driving style and conditions, with the Vredestein tyres reportedly wearing much faster than the Bridgestones. Look for a good-quality brand in any case, and check the owners' forums online for more advice on the performance of different compounds.

Brakes   4   3   2   1

There is refreshingly little to worry about here. The RX-8's relatively light weight stands in its favour, and the thick OEM brake pads wear reasonably well. Some cars have been known to squeal when braking, but this can sometimes be overcome by the simple expedient of applying the brakes harder a few times. You should nonetheless check the condition of the brakes: at the front, it is easier to inspect the callipers and pads by turning the steering to full lock on each side. The seller may also be able to show you receipts or invoices, corroborating when the pads and/or discs (rotors) were last changed. If you see any signs of engine oil near the brakes, check the oil cooler lines in the engine bay for signs of corrosion.

Underbody   4   3   2   1

Unless you are buying from a dealer with its own workshop on the premises, you will need to turn to a professional to inspect the car on a ramp or over an inspection pit. That is highly recommended, however, as it is the best way to judge the overall condition of the suspension, exhaust system and chassis. The front subframe is a notable weak spot on the RX-8, and may need to be replaced and then powder-coated for protection. Have a look too at the condition of the catalytic converter: this sits quite low and can be damaged when the car is driven over speed bumps. Be particularly vigilant when looking at personal imports from Japan, as many domestic market cars were poorly protected, if at all, when new.

Replacement front subframe, painted for protection.

Professional inspection

However well you know the RX-8, it can be hard to identify all the possible faults on a car when it is parked outside the seller's home or dealership. If you have any doubts, get the car looked over in a professional workshop, ideally one which specialises in Mazda's rotary-engined cars. No genuine seller should object to you doing this, provided of course that you cover any costs involved.

A visit to a Mazda dealership will let you check the car's service record and what recall work – which dealers were incentivised to complete – was carried out.

Nothing beats getting a car on a lift for a professional examination. (Courtesy Mazda)

Compression test

If you have any lingering doubts about the health of the engine on the car you are viewing, ask to have a compression test carried out. This can be particularly helpful on the R3: the uprated starter motor fitted to this model may mean that it continues to start satisfactorily when hot and conceals apex seal wear problems for much longer. These tests require a special type of compression tester (from Mazda or other specialists), as conventional test equipment will not give correct readings. Even if none of the serious symptoms described above are present, it may alert you to problems in store ... or give you the reassurance you are seeking!

Special compression tester from Mazda for rotary engines.

Evaluation procedure

Add up the total points from each section. Score: 120 = perfect; 90 = good; 60 = average; 30 = buyer beware! Cars scoring over 90 should be completely usable and require the minimum of repair or rectification, although continued service maintenance and care will be required to keep them in good condition. Cars scoring between 60 and 89 will require serious work (at much the same cost regardless of score). Cars scoring between 30 and 59 will require very careful assessment of the repair costs needed, especially if major engine work is required.

10 Auctions
– sold! Another way to buy your dream

Auction pros & cons
Pros: Prices are often lower than those of dealers or private sellers, and you might grab a real bargain on the day. Auctioneers have usually established clear title with the seller. At the venue you can usually examine documentation relating to the vehicle.
Cons: You have to rely on a sketchy catalogue description of condition & history. The opportunity to inspect is limited, and you cannot drive the car. Auction cars are often a little below par and may require some work. It's easy to overbid. There will usually be a buyer's premium to pay in addition to the auction hammer price.

Which auction?
Auctions by established auctioneers are advertised in car magazines and on the auction houses' websites. A catalogue, or a simple printed list of the lots for auctions might only be available a day or two ahead, though often lots are listed and pictured on auctioneers' websites much earlier. Contact the auction company to ask if previous auction selling prices are available as this is useful information (details of past sales are often available on websites).

Catalogue, entry fee, and payment details
When you purchase the catalogue of vehicles in an auction, it often acts as a ticket allowing two people to attend the viewing days and the auction. Catalogue details tend to be comparatively brief, but will include information such as 'one owner from new, low mileage, full service history,' etc. It will also usually show a guide price to give you some idea of what to expect to pay and will tell you what is charged as a 'Buyer's premium.' The catalogue will also contain details of acceptable forms of payment. At the fall of the hammer an immediate deposit is usually required, the balance payable within 24 hours. If the plan is to pay by cash, there may be a cash limit. Some auctions will accept payment by debit card. Sometimes credit or charge cards are acceptable, but will often incur an extra charge. A bank draft or bank transfer will have to be arranged in advance with your own bank, as well as with the auction house. No car will be released before **all** payments are cleared. If delays occur in payment transfers, then storage costs can accrue.

Buyer's premium
A buyer's premium will be added to the hammer price: **don't** forget this in your calculations. It is not usual for there to be a further state tax or local tax on the purchase price and/or on the buyer's premium.

Viewing
In some instances, it's possible to view on the day, or days before, as well as in the hours prior to, the auction. There are auction officials available who are willing to help out by opening engine and luggage compartments and to allow you to inspect the interior. While the officials may start the engine for you, a test drive is out of the question. Crawling under and around the car as much as you want is permitted, but you can't suggest that the car you are interested in be jacked up, or attempt to do the job yourself. You can also ask to see any documentation available.

Bidding

Before you take part in the auction, decide your maximum bid – and stick to it! It may take a while for the auctioneer to reach the lot you are interested in, so use that time to observe how other bidders behave. When it's the turn of your car, attract the auctioneer's attention and make an early bid. The auctioneer will then look to you for a reaction every time another bid is made, usually the bids will be in fixed increments until the bidding slows, when smaller increments will often be accepted before the hammer falls. If you want to withdraw from the bidding, make sure the auctioneer understands your intentions – a vigorous shake of the head when he or she looks to you for the next bid should do the trick!

Assuming that you are the successful bidder, the auctioneer will note your card or paddle number, and from that moment on you will be responsible for the vehicle.

If the car is unsold, either because it failed to reach the reserve or because there was little interest, it may be possible to negotiate with the owner, via the auctioneers, after the sale is over.

Successful bid

There are two more items to think about. How to get the car home, and insurance. If you can't drive the car, your own or a hired trailer is one way, another is to have the vehicle shipped using the facilities of a local company. The auction house will also have details of companies specialising in the transfer of cars.

Insurance for immediate cover can usually be purchased on site, but it may be more cost-effective to make arrangements with your own insurance company in advance, and then call to confirm the full details.

eBay & other online auctions

eBay & other online auctions could land you a car at a bargain price, though you'd be foolhardy to bid without examining the car first, something most vendors encourage. A useful feature of eBay is that the geographical location of the car is shown, so you can narrow your choices to those within a realistic radius of home. Be prepared to be outbid in the last few moments of the auction. Remember, your bid is binding and that it will be very, very difficult to get restitution in the case of a crooked vendor fleecing you – *caveat emptor!*

Be aware that some cars offered for sale in online auctions are 'ghost' cars. **Don't** part with **any** cash without being sure that the vehicle does actually exist and is as described (usually pre-bidding inspection is possible).

Auctioneers

Barrett-Jackson www.barrett-jackson.com
Bonhams www.bonhams.com
British Car Auctions (BCA) www.bca-europe.com/www.british-car-auctions.co.uk
Cheffins www.cheffins.co.uk
Christies www.christies.com
Coys www.coys.co.uk
eBay www.eBay.com
H&H www.classic-auctions.co.uk
RM www.rmauctions.com
Shannons www.shannons.com.au
Silver www.silverauctions.com

11 Paperwork
– correct documentation is essential!

The paper trail

Enthusiasts' cars often come with a large portfolio of paperwork accumulated by a succession of proud owners. This documentation represents the real history of the car and shows the level of care the car has received, how it's been used, which specialists have worked on it, and the dates of major repairs. As their prices have fallen, many RX-8s have now slipped into that shadowy area where owners may have skimped on maintenance; finding an RX-8 with a comprehensive history file is already a great start. Be especially wary of cars with little paperwork to support claims of major work, such as an engine rebuild.

Registration documents

All countries/states have some form of registration for private vehicles, whether it's like the American 'pink slip' system, or the British 'log book' system.

It is essential to check that the registration document is genuine, that it relates to the car in question, and that all the vehicle's details are correctly recorded, including chassis/VIN and engine numbers (if these are shown). If you are buying from the previous owner, his or her name and address will be recorded in the document; this will not be the case if you are buying from a dealer.

In the UK, the current (Euro-aligned) registration document is named 'V5C,' and is printed in coloured sections of blue, green and pink. The blue section relates to the car specification, the green section has details of the new owner and the pink

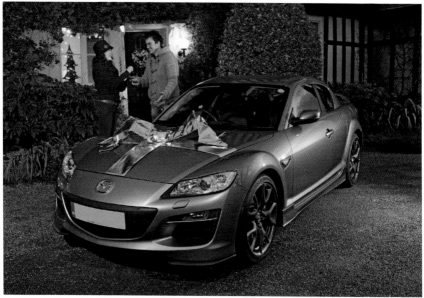

A wonderful present ... but is the paperwork in order? (Courtesy Mazda)

section is sent to the DVLA in the UK when the car is sold. A small section in yellow deals with selling the car within the motor trade.

In the UK, the DVLA will provide details of earlier keepers of the vehicle upon payment of a small fee, and much can be learned in this way.

If the car has a foreign registration, there may be expensive and time-consuming formalities to complete. Do you really want the hassle?

Roadworthiness certificate

Most country/state administrations require that vehicles are regularly tested to prove that they are safe to use on the public highway and do not produce excessive emissions. In the UK, that test (the 'MoT') is carried out at approved testing stations, for a fee. In the USA, the requirement varies, but most states insist on an emissions test every two years as a minimum, while the police are charged with pulling over unsafe-looking vehicles.

In the UK, the test is required on an annual basis once a vehicle becomes three years old. Of particular relevance for older cars is that the certificate issued includes the mileage reading recorded at the test date and, therefore, becomes an independent record of that car's history. Ask the seller if previous certificates are available. Without an MoT, the vehicle should be trailered to its new home, unless you insist that a valid MoT is part of the deal. (Not such a bad idea this, as at least you will know the car was roadworthy on the day it was tested – and you don't need to wait for the old certificate to expire before having the test done.)

Road licence

The administration of nearly every country/state charges some kind of tax for the use of its road system, the actual form of the 'road licence' and, how it is displayed, varying enormously country to country and state to state.

Whatever the form of the 'road licence', it must relate to the vehicle carrying it, and must be present and valid if the car is to be driven on the public highway legally. The value of the licence will depend on the length of time it will continue to be valid.

Changed legislation in the UK means that the seller of a car must surrender any existing road fund licence, and it is the responsibility of the new owner to re-tax the vehicle at the time of purchase and before the car can be driven on the road. It's therefore vital to see the Vehicle Registration Certificate (V5C) at the time of purchase, and to have access to the New Keeper Supplement (V5C/2), allowing the buyer to obtain road tax immediately.

If the car is untaxed because it has not been used for a period of time, the owner has to inform the licensing authorities, otherwise the vehicle's date-related registration number will be lost and there will be a painful amount of paperwork to get it re-registered.

Valuation certificate

Although the RX-8 is quite modern, the vendor may have a recent valuation certificate, or letter signed by a recognised expert stating how much he, or she, believes the particular car to be worth (such documents, together with photos, are usually needed to get 'agreed value' insurance). Generally, such documents should act only as confirmation of your own assessment of the car rather than a guarantee of value. The easiest way to find out how to obtain a formal valuation is to contact the owners' club.

Service history

Some routine servicing work, such as oil and filter changes, may have been carried out at home by enthusiastic (and hopefully capable) owners. Major work on the rotary engine, however, requires specialist tools and knowledge, so it is likely that this will have been carried out by Mazda dealers or, increasingly, by independent specialists. In any case, try to obtain as much service history and other paperwork pertaining to the car as you can. Naturally, dealer stamps, or specialist garage receipts score most points in the value stakes. For cars serviced within Mazda's official dealer network, the dealer should be able to provide you with a printout from the car's Digital Service Record (DSR). However, anything helps in the great authenticity game, items like the original bill of sale, handbook, parts invoices and repair bills adding to the story and the character of the car. Even a brochure correct to the year of the car's manufacture is a useful document and something that you could well have to search hard to locate in future years. If the seller asserts that the car has a rebuilt or replacement engine, then expect receipts and other evidence from a specialist workshop.

If the seller claims to have carried out regular servicing, ask what work was completed, when, and seek some evidence of it being carried out. Your assessment of the car's overall condition should tell you whether the seller's claims are genuine.

Restoration photographs

The RX-8 is still too new for any cars to have undergone a complete restoration, and its low value today would make this uneconomic in any case. You may well find cars, however, which have received major bodywork repairs after an accident, or been fitted with a new or rebuilt engine. If the seller tells you that the car has been undergone significant work, ask to be shown a series of photographs taken while the work was under way. These should help you gauge the thoroughness of the work. If you buy the car, ask if you can have all the photographs as they form an important part of the vehicle's history. It's surprising how many sellers are happy to part with their car and accept your cash, but want to hang on to their photographs! In the latter event, you may be able to persuade the vendor to get a set of copies made.

www.velocebooks.com / www.veloce.co.uk
Details of all current books • New book news • Special offers • Gift vouchers • Forum

48

12 What's it worth?

– let your head rule your heart

Condition

If the car you've been looking at is really bad, you've probably not bothered to use the marking system in Chapter 9 – 60-minute evaluation. You may not have even got as far as using that chapter at all!

If you did use the marking system in Chapter 9, you'll know whether the car is in Excellent (maybe concours), Good, Average or Poor condition or, perhaps, somewhere in-between these categories.

Many enthusiasts' car magazines run a regular price guide. If you haven't bought the latest editions, do so now and compare their suggested values for the model you are thinking of buying; also look at the auction prices they're reporting. The values published in the magazines tend to vary from one magazine to another, as do their scales of condition, so read carefully the guidance notes they provide. Bear in mind that a car which is truly a recent show-winner could be worth more than the highest scale published. Assuming that the car you have in mind is not in show/concours condition, relate the level of condition that you judge the car to be in with the appropriate guide price. How does the figure compare with the asking price? Before you start haggling with the seller, consider what affect any variation from standard specification might have on the car's value. If you are buying from a dealer, remember there will be a dealer's premium on the price.

In the case of the RX-8, secondhand prices have been falling markedly for some time, especially in the UK, where all the cars are now out of warranty, and expensive engine work is inevitable for many owners. Mazda's extended powertrain warranty (8 years/100,000 miles) has helped maintain prices in the USA, but as that comes to an end, prices there could well fall, too.

At some point, though, prices will likely bottom out and begin to rise again as the RX-8's collector status is recognised. Show cars like the RX-Vision concept, and important anniversaries, such as the original Cosmo's 50th birthday in 2017 or Mazda's centenary in 2020, will all turn the spotlight on Mazda's other rotary-engined cars, including the RX-8, and potentially lift value.

Desirable options/extras

Outside Japan, nearly all RX-8 models came well-equipped as standard. All cars in the UK (whether Standard or High Power) came with air-conditioning, a premium Bose audio system and 18in alloy wheels, and nearly all had leather upholstery. The High Power versions added xenon headlamps. Safety features included ABS brakes, traction control (TCS) and Dynamic Stability Control (DCS), Mazda's version of ESP.

High-quality Bose audio system. (Courtesy Mazda)

Most first-generation cars came with these 18in alloy wheels. (Courtesy Mazda)

In the USA, Sport, Touring and Grand Touring Packages progressively added these key features: xenon headlamps, DSC and 18in wheels (Sport), sunroof and Bose audio system (Touring) and heated, power-operated leather seats (Grand Touring). Avoid base-spec cars (which are rare in any case), then focus on condition rather than specific options.

Undesirable features

Automatic transmission has limited appeal on this model.

Be very cautious when looking at modified cars, such as those which have been supercharged. Unless the work has been carried out by a specialist whose work you know, and using parts from reputable suppliers, these changes could be more trouble than they are worth, and make the car harder to sell on.

The satnav system was a desirable option when the car was new, but its presentation now appears very old-fashioned. Updated maps have not been produced for some time. Moreover, there have been reports of the units causing battery drain issues as they fail to close down completely. You'll be better off buying an aftermarket satnav.

The sunroof is also a mixed blessing, as it eats into headroom (by as much as 75mm/3in), which may be an issue if you are tall or wear a helmet on track days.

An unusual combination: tan and black leather in a US-market automatic. (Courtesy Mazda)

Optional satnav in a first-generation UK car. (Courtesy Mazda)

Striking a deal

Negotiate on the basis of your condition assessment, mileage, and fault rectification cost. Also take into account the car's specification. Be realistic about the value, but don't be completely intractable: a small compromise on the part of the vendor or buyer will often facilitate a deal at little real cost.

13 Do you really want to restore?
– it'll take longer and cost more than you think

The RX-8 isn't really a candidate for the kind of full-scale restoration you might undertake on an older car with classic status. It is still too new, and the cost of a complete restoration will be too expensive to make economic sense. With nearly 80,000 cars sold new in North America and more than 25,000 in the UK, there are still plenty of other cars from which to choose.

You may, however, find some cars which have suffered serious accident damage and where the repairs would be too expensive for an insurance company to approve, but which can be purchased very cheaply and returned to roadworthy condition. Keep in mind, though, that it's unlikely that you will recoup your costs: potential buyers will always be apprehensive when you come to sell on cars like these.

Rebuilding or replacing the engine

By far the more common question, however, will be whether to buy a car as a project which needs a new or rebuilt engine. Many guides in this series will urge you to steer clear of cars needing such major work. But once again, Mazda's RX-8 isn't like other cars. The exact timing and circumstances will vary by car, but replacing or rebuilding the rotary engine is pretty much inevitable.

In the USA, you can still find cars covered by Mazda's extended powertrain warranty (8 years/100,000 miles), making it much easier to avoid – or at least put off – answering this question.

In the UK, you may also decide to look for a late-model, low mileage car; if you don't plan on covering too many miles in it, you have a better chance of enjoying it for some time before major engine work becomes inescapable.

If your budget only stretches to an older or higher-mileage car, however, what should you do? One alternative is to look for a car which has already received a new or rebuilt engine, installed by a reputable specialist or experienced Mazda dealer. The purchase price will be a bit higher, but you'll be buying peace of mind for many thousands of miles to come.

Increasingly though, the cars which fill the classified ads are for vehicles which are now off the road or running badly. In other words, they need a new engine, but their current owner is unable or unwilling to pay for this work. These cars are often so cheap (less than ●x1000 in the UK) that – if the rest of the car is sound – fitting a replacement or rebuilt engine can be a viable alternative. In Europe, Mazda itself will only supply complete replacement engines: as a minimum, reckon on ●x3400, plus at least ten hours' labour to fit it. Independent specialists (see Chapter 16) offer different levels of rebuild, with prices typically from ●x2000-3500.

Rotor and housing on the workbench.

14 Paint problems
– bad complexion, including dimples, pimples and bubbles

Paint faults generally occur due to lack of protection/maintenance, or poor preparation prior to a respray or touch-up. Some of the following conditions may be present in the car you're looking at:

Orange peel
This appears as an uneven paint surface, similar to the skin of an orange. This fault – which is quite common on the RX-8, particularly on solid colours – is caused by the failure of atomized paint droplets to flow into each other when they hit the surface. It's sometimes possible to rub out the effect with proprietary paint cutting/rubbing compound or very fine grades of abrasive paper. A respray may be necessary in severe cases. Consult a bodywork repairer/paint shop for advice on the particular car.

Cracking
Severe cases are likely to have been caused by too heavy an application of paint (or filler beneath the paint). Also, insufficient stirring of the paint before application can lead to the components being improperly mixed, and cracking can result. Incompatibility with the paint already on the panel can have a similar effect. To rectify the problem, it is necessary to rub down to a smooth, sound finish before respraying the problem area.

Velocity Red Mica was the signature paint finish when the RX-8 was launched.

Crazing

Sometimes the paint takes on a crazed rather than a cracked appearance when the problems mentioned under 'Cracking' are present. This problem can also be caused by a reaction between the underlying surface and the paint. Paint removal and respraying the problem area is usually the only solution.

Paint bubbles often form along the rear wheelarches on the RX-8.

Blistering

Almost always caused by corrosion of the metal beneath the paint. Usually perforation will be found in the metal and the damage will usually be worse than that suggested by the area of blistering. The metal will have to be repaired before repainting.

Micro blistering

Usually the result of an economy respray where inadequate heating has allowed moisture to settle on the car before spraying. Consult a paint specialist, but usually damaged paint will have to be removed before partial or full respraying. Can also be caused by car covers that don't 'breathe.'

Fading

Some colours, especially reds, are prone to fading if subjected to strong sunlight for long periods without the benefit of polish protection. Sometimes proprietary paint restorers and/or paint cutting/rubbing compounds will retrieve the situation. Often a respray is the only real solution.

Peeling

Often a problem with metallic paintwork when the sealing lacquer becomes damaged and begins to peel off. Poorly applied paint may also peel. The remedy is to strip and start again!

Dimples

Dimples in the paintwork are caused by the residue of polish (particularly silicone types) not being removed properly before respraying. Paint removal and repainting is the only solution.

Dents

Small dents are usually easily cured by the 'Dentmaster' or equivalent process, that sucks or pushes out the dent (as long as the paint surface is still intact). Companies offering dent removal services usually come to your home: consult your telephone directory.

15 Problems due to lack of use

– just like their owners, RX-8s need exercise!

With many RX-8s off the road awaiting engine repairs, it's very likely you'll come across a car which has not been driven for some time. Like any car, the RX-8 needs to be driven for at least 20 miles once a week, so that all the fluids are thoroughly warmed through. And driven hard! Low revs won't let you enjoy the rotary engine, and will do it no good – too many low-speed journeys will lead to the build-up of harmful carbon deposits.

Corroded brake discs on a car left standing outdoors.

Seized and rusted components

Pistons in callipers, slave and master cylinders can seize.

The clutch may seize if the plate becomes stuck to the flywheel because of corrosion.

Handbrakes (parking brakes) can seize if the cables and linkages rust. On the RX-8, the brake discs are particularly liable to surface corrosion if the car has been left standing outdoors.

Fluids

All fluids should be replaced at regular intervals. Uninhibited coolant can corrode internal waterways. Lack of the correct mix of antifreeze can cause serious damage to the engine. Silt settling and solidifying can cause overheating.

Brake fluid absorbs water from the atmosphere and should be renewed every two years.

Check the DOT code on the tyres.

Tyre problems

Tyres that have had the weight of the car on them in a single position for some time will develop flat spots, resulting in some (usually temporary) vibration. The tyre walls may have cracks or (blister-type) bulges, meaning new tyres are needed. Even if the tyres appear to be in good condition, check the date of manufacture: the DOT code on the sidewall will show you the week and year of manufacture. The tyre in the photo is from week 22 of year (20)10. At more than five years old, the tread compound will already be hardening and the performance of the tyre will be affected.

Shock absorbers (dampers)

With lack of use, the dampers will lose their elasticity, or even seize. Creaking, groaning and stiff suspension are signs of this problem.

Rubber and plastic

Radiator hoses may have perished and split, possibly resulting in the loss of all coolant. Window, door and rear light seals can all harden and leak. Gaiters and boots can crack. Wiper blades will harden.

Electrics

The battery will be of little use if it has not been charged for many months. If a car is left standing for several weeks, connecting it to a trickle charger will keep it in good condition.

Earthing/grounding problems are common when the connections have corroded. Wiring insulation can harden and fail.

Rotting exhaust system

Exhaust gas contains a high water content so exhaust systems corrode very quickly from the inside when the car is not used. This even applies to stainless steel systems.

16 The Community
– key people, organisations and companies in the RX-8 world

As the RX-8 grows older, and with no immediate replacement for it, there are fewer and fewer official Mazda dealers who are able to look after its unique rotary engine, particularly in Europe. Fortunately, many independent specialists have stepped into this space; some of them have worked on rotaries ever since the first RX-7 was launched in 1978. Flourishing owners' clubs and online forums in both Europe and the USA also mean that friendly advice from knowledgeable enthusiasts is never far away.

Rotary specialists: parts, servicing and rebuilds
This is only a partial list, so check with the owners' clubs, and online, for other specialists near you. Some of the UK workshops listed, such as Rotary Revs, also sell high-quality parts, such as coil packs, as an alternative to OEM parts. In North America, there is a wider range of workshops which can maintain the RX-8 – the owners' club or the parts specialists listed below should be able to advise you for your state/province.

UK
Apex Rotary, Alton (Hampshire): www.apexrotary.com
Hayward Rotary, Newbury (Berkshire): www.haywardrotary.co.uk
Hurley Engineering, Coventry (West Midlands): www.hurleyrotary.com
LC Rotary, Orpington (Kent): www.lcrotary.co.uk
Rotary Revs, Birstall (West Yorkshire): http://rotaryrevs.com
Rx Motors, Salisbury (Wiltshire): http://rxmotors.co.uk
TW White & Sons, Byfleet (Surrey) – originally the largest RX-8 dealer in Europe and UK importer of automatic cars: www.twwhiteandsons.co.uk
WGT Auto Developments, Middlewich (Cheshire): www.wgtautodevelopments.co.uk

USA
Black Halo Racing: http://black-halo-racing.myshopify.com
Pettit Racing: http://shop.pettitracing.com
Racing Beat: www.racingbeat.com

Clubs and online forums
The RX-8 is truly a car of the Internet generation, with excellent support online. The biggest groups include:

Ireland – Irish Rotary: http://irishrotary.com/forum/
UK – RX-8 Owners' club UK: www.rx8ownersclub.co.uk
USA – RX-8Club.com: www.rx8club.com

Events
The owners' clubs regularly organise social and track day meetings, which can be a great way to meet existing owners and find out more about the cars. In the UK, the RX-8 is usually well represented at 'Simply Japanese' at Beaulieu, and at the annual 'JapFest' shows.

Track day action at a Prodrive-sponsored event. (Courtesy Mazda)

Books and magazines

Two books dedicated to the RX-8 were published when the model was introduced. They provide a good overview of Mazda's history and the development of the RX-8:

Mazda RX-8, Jack Yamaguchi (Ring Ltd, 2003)
Mazda RX-8, Ray Hutton & others (Delius Klasing with Mazda Motor Europe, 2003)

The RX-8 also appears regularly in the pages of two magazines dedicated to Japanese performance cars and tuning, *Japanese Performance* and *Banzai*.

www.velocebooks.com / www.veloce.co.uk
Details of all current books • New book news • Special offers • Gift vouchers • Forum

57

17 Vital statistics

– essential data at your fingertips

Production figures

A total of 193,094 RX-8s were built, across both generations and all models.

Technical specifications

Engine

Engine capacity (all models): two rotors, each of 654cc = 1308cc. Nominally equivalent to 2616cc piston engine for UK registration purposes.

Power and torque output (quoted by Mazda)

	UK		USA (SAE figures)			
	Standard Power (first-gen) five-speed manual	High Power & R3 six-speed manual	First-gen six-speed manual	Second-gen six-speed manual	First-gen four-speed auto	six-speed auto with six-port engine
Peak power	189bhp @7000rpm	228bhp @8200rpm	238hp @8500rpm	232hp @8500rpm	197hp @7200rpm	212hp @7500rpm
Maximum torque	162lb-ft @5000rpm	156lb-ft @5500rpm	159lb-ft @5500rpm	159lb-ft @5500rpm	164lb-ft @5000rpm	159lb-ft @5500rpm
Redline	7500rpm	9000rpm	9000rpm	9000rpm	7500rpm	7500rpm

Transmission

In the UK, the five-speed manual transmission was fitted to Standard Power cars, the six-speed to High Power cars.

In the USA, the four-speed automatic transmission was replaced by the six-speed in October 2006.

Final drive ratios

	First-generation	Second-generation
Manual: five-speed	4.444	NA
Manual: six-speed	4.444	4.777
Automatic: four-speed	4.444	NA
Automatic: six-speed	4.300	4.300

Performance figures

Top speed: 146mph (235km/h)

Acceleration 0-60mph (96km/h): 6.5 seconds

Figures quoted are for R3 version, tested by *evo* magazine in 2008.

Suspension

Double-wishbone front suspension.

Multi-link (five-link) rear suspension.

Uprated suspension on Mazdaspeed, 40th Anniversary, PZ, Shinka, R3 and Spirit R models.

Steering
Rack and pinion, with electric power assistance on all models.
Turns lock-to-lock: 3.0
Turning circle (kerb-to-kerb): 10.6m (34.8ft)

Brakes
Ventilated discs front and rear on all models.
ABS (Anti-lock Braking System) with EBD (Electronic Brake-force Distribution).

Wheels & tyres

Alloy wheels	Tyres	Application
16in	225/55 R16	Fitted to base-spec cars in USA and personal imports
18in	225/45 R18	Fitted to most first-generation cars
19in	225/40 R19	Available on second-generation cars

Electrical equipment

Models	First-generation	Second-generation
Battery	12V 70AH	12V 80D/26L
Starter	12V, 1.4kW	12V, 2.0kW

Dimensions: all models

Length	4435mm (174.6in)
Width	1770mm (69.7in)
Height	1340mm (52.8in)
Wheelbase	2700mm (106.3in)
Kerb weight (without driver)	1354-1411kg (2985-3111lb), depending on model
Luggage capacity	2.9m³ (10.2ft³)

Filling capacities

Models	First-generation	Second-generation
Fuel tank	61 litres (16.1 US gal)	65 litres (17.2 US gal)
Engine oil	190: 6.1 litres (6.4 US quarts)	7.0 litres (7.4 US quarts)
	230: 6.9 litres (7.3 US quarts)	

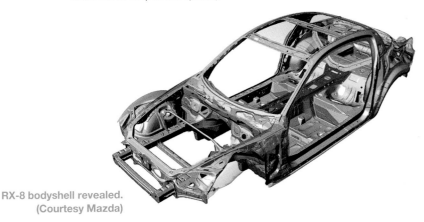

RX-8 bodyshell revealed.
(Courtesy Mazda)

The Essential Buyer's Guide™ series ...

Also from Veloce Publishing ...

Mazda MX-5 Miata
The 'Mk1' NA-series 1988 to 1997
Brian Long

This is the definitive history of the first generation Mazda MX-5 – also known as the Miata or Eunos Roadster. A fully revised version of an old favourite, now focussing on the NA series, this book covers all major markets, and includes stunning contemporary photography gathered from all over the world.

ISBN: 978-1-845847-78-4
Hardback • 25x20.7cm
• £30* UK/$50* USA •
144 pages • 221 pictures

Mazda MX-5 Miata
1.6 Enthusiast's Workshop Manual
Rod Grainger

Friendly & easy to understand. Covers all 1989-1994 1.6 models, inc. Eunos. Rod stripped down an MX-5 in a domestic garage using ordinary tools & took over 1500 step-by-step photos. details every aspect of important jobs.

ISBN: 978-1-845840-83-9
Paperback • 27x21cm •
£30* UK/$59.95* USA •
368 pages • 1600 pictures

Index